Order this book online at www.trafford.com
or email orders@trafford.com

Most Trafford titles are also available at major online book retailers.

Printed in the United States of America.

ISBN: 978-1-4907-3610-5 (*sc*)
ISBN: 978-1-4907-3609-9 (*e*)

Library of Congress Control Number: 2014908661

Trafford rev. 05/13/2014

 www.trafford.com

North America & international
toll-free: 1 888 232 4444 (USA & Canada)
fax: 812 355 4082

BIBLE CITATION
NEW KING JAMES VERSION

Sincere REFLECTIONS

A Compilation of Prose and Poetry

by

BILL BURGOYNE

Table of Contents

I believe in God, the Father Almighty, Creator of Heaven and Earth and Hell and everything in between. I believe in Jesus Christ, His only Son, begotten not made, one in being with the Father. Jesus Christ has many brothers and sisters – Mohammed and Buddha to name a few.

I believe in the Truth, painful though it may be. One thing about the Truth is that it's constant, even though it's perceived by many people in many different ways. Once people believed the Earth was flat, but the Truth is that it's elliptical in shape. Only Columbus knew for sure, I think.

Once I told my wife the Truth about me. She couldn't deal with it. She became so angry she divorced me – and rightfully so. The words of Jesus are indeed true for me: "And you will know the Truth, and the Truth will set you free." (John 8:32). Today, I'm free indeed. Free from living a double life. Free from sexual perversions. Free from stress. Free from pain Free from doubts and confusion.

I believe in freedom. Freedom to speak the Truth, even though it hurts. Freedom to pursue happiness and attain it at the same time. Freedom to live in peace, accepting all of humanity as family, regardless of their beliefs and customs and even their behaviors. Can terrorism be excused? Absolutely not. But it can be forgiven, with time. Terrorists are terrorists because they've been trained to be. They are driven to it by the same force that drove me to sexual perversions. But there is a force that can indeed conquer it. That force is Love.

I believe in Love. Love for humanity. Love for all of God's creations. Love of nature. Love of all animals, plants, and even insects, like ants and mosquitoes and bees and spiders and houseflies.

I believe in the Holy Spirit of Love, and I believe that Holy Spirit of God is a woman.

I believe this because I believe in the TRUTH of God's Word which says: "Then God said: 'Let Us make man in Our image, according to Our likeness; let them have dominion over the fish of the sea, over the birds of the air, over the cattle, over all the earth and over every creeping thing that creeps on the earth.'

So God created man in His own image; in the image of God He created him; *male and female* He created them." (Genesis 1:26-27). And because God's Word says "Let Us make man," I believe that God consists of 3 divine Beings. I believe that God is a holy Trinity of Beings, united together as one God because I believe in the following scripture verses: "In the beginning was the Word and the Word was with God, and the Word was God." (John 1:1). I believe that the Word was Jesus Christ because God's Word says that it was the Word who became flesh: "And the Word became flesh and dwelt among us, and we beheld His Glory, the Glory as of the only be-gotten of the Father, full of Grace and Truth." (John 1:14).

I believe that the Father of Jesus is God because I believe this: "Grace to you in peace from God our Father and the Lord, Jesus Christ." (Philippians 1:2). And I believe that the Holy Spirit is God because I believe this: "But Peter said: 'Ananias, why has Satan filled your heart to *lie to the Holy Spirit* and keep back part of the price of the land for yourself?

While it remained was it not your own? And after it was sold, was it not in your own control? Why have you conceived this thing in your heart? *You have not lied to men, but to God!*'" (Acts 5:3-4).

God's Word tells us all about the roles that the Holy Spirit plays in our lives: Our Teacher, our Counselor, and so on, but nowhere does it tell us who She is, or what Her name is! So one night in prayer, I asked Her what Her name was. She told me that Her name was Grace!

And this is who She is: She is the Personification of the unconditional and perfect Love of God that exists between the Father and the Son, and all of us! It is no wonder why God's Word says that : "My Grace is sufficient for you, for My strength is made perfect in your weakness!" (2 Corinthians 12:9).

I believe that God's Grace is the only hope that remains for this troubled world of ours. She is the only hope that we have of overcoming any temptation or of obeying any of God's commands!

I also believe that there are 3 distinct Persons in the Trinity who is God because I believe this: "For there are three that bear witness in heaven: the Father, the Word, and the Holy Spirit, and these three are One!" (1 John 5:7). If the Father is a Person and the Son is a Person, then it must follow the the Holy Spirit is a Person also – otherwise they would not be One!

I believe that God still performs miracles today, just like He always has and will continue to do as people honor His existence, because I believe in the following scripture verse: "Jesus Christ is the same yesterday, today, and forever." (Hebrews 13:8).

I believe that anyone can accomplish anything that they strive to do with persistence, perseverance, self-discipline, and practice, provided that they trust and believe that God will help them to do so because I believe in the following scripture verse: "Jesus looked at them intently and said: 'Humanly speaking it is impossible, but with God, everything is possible." (Matthew 19:26).

I believe in having the courage to stand up for what we believe in and express our beliefs without fear of retribution by the powers that be. I believe this because I believe in the following scripture verse: "For God hath not given us the spirit of fear; but of power, and of love, and of a sound mind."(II Timothy 1:7). I believe that everyone is entitled to receive anything their hearts desire, provided that they believe or have faith in the Truth of the following scripture verse: "Whatever you ask for in prayer, believing, you shall receive." (Matthew 21:22).

I believe that God's angels constantly watch over us and protect us from any calamity because I believe in the following scripture verse: "And He will command His angels concerning you that they guard you in all your ways, They will lift you up in their hands so you don't strike your foot against a stone." (Psalm 91:11-12).

I believe that God always keeps His promises without fail. Not so for many of us humans, however hard we may try. The best policy is to never make a promise that you don't intend to keep. This is best because I believe in the following scripture verse: "When you make a promise to God, don't delay in fulfilling it. He has no pleasure in fools! Fulfill your promise. It is better not to make a promise and not fulfill it." (Ecclesiastes 5:4-5).

I believe in developing strong relationships with people of other faiths, cultures, and governments so that world peace can be finally achieved without bloodshed. In this way, our perceived enemies can become our friends if we treat them as such. I believe in Love! I believe that God is Love! This is because

I believe in the following scripture verse: "But to you who are willing to listen, I say, Love your enemies! Do good to those who hate you. Bless those who curse you! Pray for those who hurt you!" (Luke 6:27-28).

This is why Jesus gave us this one last command: "This is My commandment: That you Love one another as I have Loved you!" (John 15:12). I also believe that any "born again" Christian can perform miracles as well because I believe in the following scripture verse: *"Verily, verily, I say unto you, they that believeth on me,* **the** *works that I do shall they do also; and greater works than these shall they do; because I go unto my Father."* (John 14:12).

I believe in you! I believe that if you only trust and believe that Jesus Christ is God, you will find success in all that you do and you can dream and hope in a future full of prosperity because I believe in the following scripture verse: "For I know the plans I have for you; plans to prosper you and not to harm you, plans to give you hope and a future." (Jeremiah 29:11).

I believe in dialogue and compromise and negotiation and win-win solutions.

I believe the Red Sox will win the world series, again. FYI-they already did! This year again! Hoorah!

I believe in the United States of America, and the republic for which it's flag stands.

I believe that the whole is greater than the sum of its parts!

I believe in optimism and hope for a better future for America and for the whole world and for me!

I believe that just as God the Father, God the Son, and God the Holy Spirit are united as 1 God, one day soon, all of God's creation will become united with Him so that we will all be one with the universe!

I believe that there is only one name for God that is higher than any other name. That name is Jesus Christ!

I believe that every religion throughout the earth, including all atheists, agnostics, and heathens, and all of God's creation will come to realize and proclaim that the name of Jesus Christ is the highest of any other name of God!

I believe this because I believe in the following scripture verse: "And every creature which is in heaven and on earth and under the earth and such as are in the sea, and all that are in them, I heard saying:

"Blessing and honor and glory and power be to Him who sits on the throne, and to the Lamb, forever and ever!"

(Revelation 5:13)

I believe in Life everlasting for all eternity. I believe that the kingdom of heaven is within us and all around us. We need only become aware of its presence!

THIS I BELIEVE!

A DROP OF WATER

Moisture was my mother's name;
My father was a cloud.
A sudden force upon me came;
The thunder – it was loud.

Lightning struck when I was born,
A clear, transparent ball;
But from my parents, I was torn;
Just how, I can't recall.

I splattered on a roadside rock;
My parents thought I'd died.
But I survived that sudden shock;
As I looked around me, and cried.

All my friends went down the drain;
And wound up in the river.
But there on the grate, I was forced to remain.
It was enough to make me shiver.

The sun came out and I disappeared.
I died I thought – 'twas what I always feared.
I looked around and all was white.
My mother would be proud, in spite.

Because I'm now a cumulus cloud.

LIFE

Life is full of ups and downs;
Tears and laughter, cops and clowns.
Some people claim to be your friends;
Betray them once, and their friendship ends.

Anger, jealousy, bitterness, and hate;
Always result when you cheat on your mate!
Sometimes they happen as a result of ill-fate;
When you come home from work just a little too late!

From love we were born into a world full of fright;
Or was it from sex on a cold winter's night.
Presidents and kings were all once just babies;
Royal commitments made from probable maybe's.

Take heart all you lovers, there's no need to worry;
There's still time for love – if you're not in a hurry!
No need to panic – go helter, skelter, and scurry;
You're loved by a Man born in a winter snow flurry.

He fills all life's valleys with mountains of love;
He flies through life's problems on the wings of a dove,
Betrayed once by Judas, He hung on a cross;
As 30 pieces of silver were flung in a toss!

A man He called Peter denied Him 3 times, it is said;
This Man who fed thousands with only 7 loaves of bread!
But Peter repented as he watched Jesus faint;
Then Jesus forgave him and today he's a saint!

THE STONE

Yesterday I was born – a mountain peak,
Shining brightly in the noon day sun.
A climber's hammer struck my face,
And I fell down into the swiftly flowing creek.

The current pushed me – I could hardly talk;
Then I married a mossy wet rock.
My son's a cliff – my daughter's a boulder;
But with the passing of years, I've grown much older.

Today I died – a grain of sand;
Slipped through the fingers of some lover's hand.

Spitefulness and sorrow, hurtfulness and hate;
All I left behind as the wind blew me through the gate.
Now I'm a diamond – a brilliant shining stone;
Forever fastly frozen in God's almighty throne.

HEAVEN'S DOOR

Waves rise up from gusts of wind;
And crash upon the shore.
Saints rise up from those who've sinned;
And knock on Heaven's door.

The sound of silence fills the air;
The lakes and winds grow calm.
The clouds are gone – the weather's fair;
As God extends His palm.

Awake – o sleeper – from the grave –
Of doubt and disbelief.
Jesus Christ your soul did save;
By dying with a thief.

Where once His body laid in state;
There's now an empty tomb.
He lives to open Heaven's gate;
To all who give Him room.

So step aside from grief and sin;
And let the gate swing wide.
His kingdom beckons from within;
And bids us come inside

.So recall the mighty gusts of wind;
That sent the waves to shore.
And turn to Jesus if you've sinned;
And walk through Heaven's Door.

THE SEEDLING

It seemed like only yesterday that I was born;
Surrounded with soil, my hard shell was torn.
What gave me courage, you'll be tempted to ask?
T''was the sun that I strove for – to reach it my task.

When I broke through the surface, I thought it was great;
Finally I made it, and not a moment too late!
The sun gave me strength and I felt so alive;
Then I burst forth a leaf and I knew I'd survive.

But then the clouds came and I shivered with fright;
How can I live when the days are dark as night?
It thundered and poured and I thought I had drowned;
No longer erect, I laid flat on the ground.
My new leaf torn and mud-covered, I struggled in vain;
I collapsed in that torrent and cursed all the rain.

I knew no tomorrow – there was only today;
Darkness and death were surely here to stay.
I slept in my sorrow and thought it my fate –
To die here in rubble – what a pitiful state!

But then something happened – it's only now I know why;
I awoke to a rainbow and a clear, cloudless sky!
Something warm surged within me and gave me new life;
Then I knew there was a purpose for all my suffering and strife!

The sun shone upon me and filled me with strength;
I hardly even noticed I had grown a full length!
The mud suddenly fell off me as if it were dust;

I was only a seedling and had years left to grow;
But today I'm an oak tree and it's great just to know;
That I'm here for a purpose I hope everyone's seeing;
To fulfill the plan of the earth's Supreme Being.

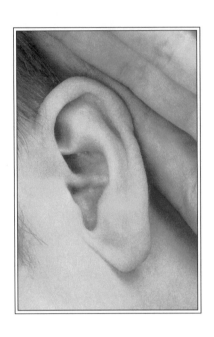

LISTEN!

Listen! Do you hear that sound? It is the sound of silence!
Listen! Do you hear that sound? It is the sound of the wind blowing!
Listen! Do you hear that sound? It is the sound of a dog barking;
Listen! Do you hear that sound? It is the sound of a man yelling:
"Be still!   Be silent!"
The dog's master is the man who holds the leash –
To which the dog's collar is fastened.

The dog barks for freedom.
But the man just yells the louder:
"Be still!   Be silent!"
The man is cold and wishes to go inside.
The man releases his leash from the dog's collar.
The dog runs free! The man goes inside.

Listen! Do you hear that sound? It is the sound of water flowing!
Listen! Do you hear that sound? It is the sound of the wind blowing;
Listen! Do you hear that sound? It is the sound of a dog resting!
Listen! Do you hear that sound? It is the sound of a man resting!
Listen! Do you hear that sound! It is the sound of a door creaking!
Listen! Do you hear that voice? It is the voice of a Lamb speaking!

RIVERS

Rivers flow throughout the earth;
As simple raindrops give them birth.
Sometimes beavers build a dam;
To try to stop their current.
Sometimes it works, sometimes it doesn't.

TO YOUR HEALTH

Once upon a midnight glowing,
Like a silver crescent river flowing;
I stood alone on the mountainside.
The stars were hidden by thunder clouds that night;
The birds a wing, as if in fright.

Satan's pride would soon be humbled.
The thunder roared – I choked and stumbled.
I fell to the ground – all empty and broken.
"Father help me!" I cried in a voice soft spoken.

The lightning crashed throughout the meadow,
And all the world could hear its echo.
Raindrops fell as I arose –
And went to the garden – I sensed my foes!

Hark! Awaken all you who are fast asleep!
The enemy comes in a deadly creep.
I felt his kiss – so blunt and cold;
The time had come – you've all been told!

A sword was drawn – an ear flew by;
My heart was pierced by that man's cry!
I touched his wound in a moment of pity;
My hands were bound as they led Me to the city.

Thirty pieces of silver lay strewn in the street;
I beheld the enemy strung up by his feet.
Friendly faces grew silent as each cock crowed;
They all disappeared as I walked down the road.

"Flog Him" they said as I went to the dungeon;
They ripped off My clothes - I cringed from the bludgeon.

When it was over, I stood there in anguish;
All the sins of humanity soon I would vanquish.

Friendly faces grew silent as each cock crowed;
They all disappeared as I walked down the road.

"A King!" they shouted as they crowned Me with thorns;
I grew weak as I thought – it's God who adorns.
Away to the court, no time for a jury;
They rushed Me away in a flurry of fury.
"Give us Barabbas!" came the cry from without;
Myriads of angels wept at the shout.
I thought I would faint from the weight of the tree;
But this cup I would swallow so you could be free.

"Get up!" yelled the soldiers, "climb up that hill!"
How blessed are they that obey My Father's will!
I lay on the ground, a cross for My bed;
As a ransom for sinners, My blood will be shed!

The sky grew dark as they drove in the last nail;
As they lifted Me up, it started to hail.
"It is finished!" I whispered when the hour was three;
I gave up My Spirit, and now all are free!
They took down My body to lay in a tomb;
They may as well have sealed My mother's womb.

Three days later, all sins to atone;
At the first ray of sunlight, I cast away the stone.
Now I sit forever on My Father's throne.

My kingdom's within you – My Spirit is too!
My Light is alive and I share It with you.
Now open your heart and your soul to It's glowing;
And a river of Light shall within you be flowing.

Every vestige of sin has by its current been drowned;
And no trace of disease shall within you be found!

LONELINESS

Loneliness comes and then it goes;
It's a feeling that thrives on personal woes;
A friend says "hello" and it seems like it's gone;
But then it comes back like a hungry new fawn.
It makes a hole in my heart that I can't seem to fill;
Unless someone comes into my life and gives me a thrill.

MOVIN'"ON

The flowing brook – the river's edge;
The birch tree on the lawn;
The old tool house with Grampy's sledge;
There's more….Should I go on?

The wood pile 'tween the willow trees;
The shack – and cookouts during winter's freeze;
Rusted ski-doos out of gas;
The tulips, daffodils, and grass.

The chainsaws echo with their hollow sound;
Bennet's bridge and pigeons, and the old town pound;
Grampy's screenhouse and spaghetti sauce;
And Kitty's apple pie;
Grandma's smile and Mizzy;
And seasons all gone by.

Memories soon they all shall be;
The price for being free…
To follow Jesus beyond His cross;
And fulfill my destiny.

THE THREE FOOLS

Three kings once journeyed from afar;
They abandoned their kingdoms to follow a star;
Through bleak frozen forests, and snow covered fields;
They came to a stable and laid down their shields.

There in a manger the infant Jesus lay snuggled in wheat;
He smiled when they entered and laid gifts at His feet.
They brought something called myrrh with frankincense and gold.
"He'll surely be King," they thought, "when He's old,"

Then they departed and went on their way;
Leaving the Infant asleep on the hay.
Their friends called them fools when they said where they'd been;
But today they're still known as "The three wise men."

WORLD PEACE

A shot rang out across the land;
A nation died upon the sand.
A baby cried upon the shore;
A mother wondered, "what's it all for?"

A trumpet sounds from east to west;
An army laughs as if in jest.
A mighty cloud above it storms;
No time now for political reforms.

A rooster crows – it's early dawn;
A sudden flash – the earth is gone!
World peace at last, but what a price;
If only we had listened to the Lord's advice.

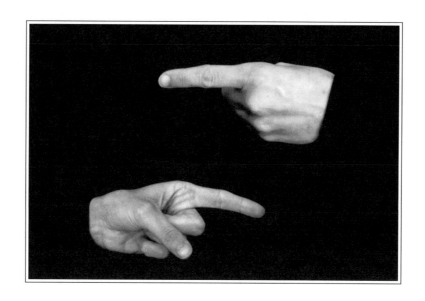

WHAT'S THE POINT?

What's the point of writing
If what's written isn't read?
What's the point of reading
If you can watch tv instead?

What's the point of listening,
if what you hear's not true?
What's the point of working,
if you don't like what you do?

What's the point of walking,
if you end up going lame?
What's the point of dreaming ,
if when wakened everything's the same!

What's the point of looking,
If what you see brings pain;
What's the point of speaking,
If what's spoken is in vain?

So if you're life is fading,
And your bones are out of joint;
Just live your life for Jesus;
If you don't, you've missed the point.

IF

If only I could live my life
Without an "if" or "but"
I finally would be free at last
To do no matter what!
If I do this – if I do that;
Then I'll be thus and so.

But don't do this or don't do that
Or else you'll surely die.
I wonder what would happen
If I only dared to try?
To do the things I once could do
But gave myself an order:
Because of pain or grief or fear
To never cross the border.

For what is pain but life unlived
A seed on rocky ground
There is no need to fear again
For fear is faith unfound.

There is a *Love* that lives for us;
Without an "if" or "but."
A *Love* that lingers on and on
To *love* no matter what

For life is simply *"Love"* unleashed
A seed on fertile soil.
There is no need to spend your life
In endless futile toil.

Give thanks to *God* with simple praise
And watch the seedling sprout
And soon all sickness will depart
Of this there is no doubt..

AGAIN

Again I rise to face the day
To go to work and make some pay
But not enough to make ends meet
So I must not yet go down in defeat.

Again I sleep to gain some rest
So that every day I'll be at my best
Again that seems not good enough
Because, for sure, there's too much stuff
To do it all and still succeed.

Again I wish we could all be freed
From having to satisfy everyone else's need
So that every moment could be filled with peace
And the tears of children all would cease.

But the very next day, I rise again
To do the same things all over again
Whether I live to work or work to live
Again and again, I must always give.

Again the dead of winter follows fall
And a great white blanket covers all.
And then the spring is born again
And so life continues without end.

SUCCESS

So many people seek to find
Success by working hard.
Life for them is a constant grind
They have seldom time to mow their yard.

They work and work to make more money
They're like little bees who just make honey
But the money comes and then it goes
While success – it still escapes them.

So why be like the busy bee
That gathers pollen to the hive?
Seek instead to be really free
There's no better way to thrive!

The eagle soars from tree to tree
It's only work is flying
It found success when it left its nest
Its only way was trying.

The seagull soars from sea to sea
Its only work is fishing
It finds success when it uses its head
For more than merely wishing.

So be like a bird and success you'll find
And money too, without the grind.
But keep in mind that in spite of the weather
The only unsuccessful bird of its kind
Is the one who has no feather.

HERE I AM

To where do I go if not from here?
For where is here with a "w" up front
Or where is there without a "t".
But if indeed I go from here,
I still have to go indeed from there.
But 3 other choices I do have:
I could go nowhere and just stay here;
Or I could go anywhere and then I'd be there!
Or I could go everywhere except from here –
No - including here!

BUGS

Bugs are curious little creatures, true;
They often wonder what to do.
Sometimes they crawl upon the floor;
Or fly in your face when you go out the door!

Why are they here, you'd be tempted to ask?
To drive us nuts, it seems is their task,
But bugs are God's creatures, no matter how small;
They live in our gardens from spring until fall.

There's two in my bedroom –
On the ceiling they crawl.
I just let them live there -
They're just bugs after all

LOVE

Love is often elusive but often sincere;
Anyone who lacks it deserves a kick in the rear;
My quest is to find it, whatever the cost;
I once thought I'd found it but, alas, it was lost;

True love is real but requires a great price;
If you're willing to pay it, the result will be nice;
Too bad you can't buy it, it's just not for sale;
God only gives it to those who don't fail….

…To earn it by giving themselves in the deal.
Then when you find it you discover it's real…
Only when given with no strings attached.

HONEYBEES

Honeybees buzz from flower to flower;
Sucking up pollen from hour to hour;
When they're all done, they buzz back to the hive;
So that during the winter, they'll all stay alive.

Honey's their product, so sweet to the taste;
But if they buzz by you, you'll high-tail it in haste;
Their sting is so nasty, it brings tears to your eyes;
To avoid it at all costs is a word to the wise.

But without them no flowers would form into fruit;
And then all of mankind would be lost in pursuit;
Pear trees and apple trees would all disappear;
A loss to us humans is what we would fear.

"For unto us a Son is given."

"And she will have a Son, and you are to name Him "Jesus."

(Matthew 1:21)

CHRISTMAS

Christmas comes just once each year;
To bring good gifts to all those who are dear;
Sometimes they're wrapped with ribbons and bows;
So that inside there's something that only Santa knows.

What's in it for me, you'll be tempted to ask;
But you'll never know until it comes into your grasp.

A trinket or toy or some new clothes to wear;
But whatever it is, you can trust it'll be there;
Even if it's invisible, like Jesus or Love
or even just air!

REFLECTIONS ON ST. VALENTINE:

VALENTINE'S DAY COMES JUST ONCE EACH YEAR,
TO CALL US TO LOVE SOMEONE WHO'S DEAR.
HIS ORIGINS ARE VAGUE AND NOT VERY CLEAR
BEATEN AND STONED WITHOUT SHEDDING A TEAR.

HE WAS BEHEADED BY CLAUDIUS IN SPITE OF HIS FEAR.
A MARTYR FOR SURE, HIS SOUL NOW DWELLS IN HEAVEN
WHERE HIS SPIRIT NOW FLOATS IN HIGH GEAR.

ALL LOVERS ADORE HIM, JUST WHY IS UNCLEAR
THEY KISS AND EMBRACE HIM AND SENSE HE IS NEAR
AND ALL THAT IS DONE WITHOUT DRINKING A BEER!

FREEDOM

FREEDOM REIGNS THROUGHOUT OUR LAND;
BETWEEN OUR SHORES OUR FLAGS STILL STAND.

A GIFT BESTOWED BY GENERATIONS PAST;
WHILE GOD'S OWN LOVE SHALL MAKE IT LAST.

THAT SOLDIERS GIVE UP THEIR LIVES FOR IT IS TRUE;
THE PRICE THEY PAID SO THEY COULD GIVE IT TO YOU.

IT'S HOW WE USE IT THAT DETERMINES OUR FATE;
BUT IF WE USE IT TO SIN, THEN IT'S NEVER TOO LATE...

TO USE IT TO PRAY TO THE GOD OF OUR CHOICE;
WHETHER YAHWEH OR ALLAH IS CAUSE TO REJOICE

THAT EVERY SIN IS FORGIVEN NO MATTER HOW GREAT;
AND JESUS WILL WALK WITH US THROUGH GOD'S PEARLY GATE.

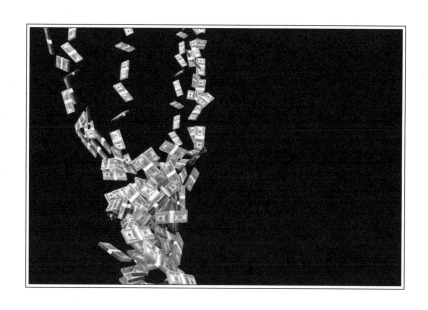

POSSESIONS

WHEN WE'RE LITTLE WE'RE GIVEN TOYS;
WE PLAY WITH THEM AND MAKE LOTS OF NOISE.

WHEN WE'RE YOUNG WE GATHER MORE;
AND WHEN THEY BREAK WE GO TO THE STORE.

WHEN WE'RE OLD WE'VE GATHERED SO MUCH;
THAT WE USE THEM ALL SO WE DON'T LOSE TOUCH.

BUT IF WE'RE POOR WE JUST HAVE SOME;
AND ALL OUR FRIENDS THINK WE'RE JUST PLAIN DUMB.

BUT EVEN IF INDEED, WE'VE LOST THEM ALL;
AND BANG OUR HEADS AGAINST THE WALL.

THEN WE'VE GOT NOTHING MORE TO LOSE;
SO WE CAN PRAY TO JESUS IF WE CHOOSE.

AND IF WE TRUST IN HIS LOVE HIS FAVOR WE'LL GAIN;
THEN ALL WE'VE LOST WOULDN'T HAVE BEEN IN VAIN.

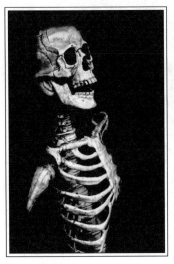

FEAR

Feeling pain is something we all dread;
To avoid it is something we'd rather do instead.

But when it comes we must endure it true;
But those who escape it are very few.

They are blessed by God's Grace alone;
So that through them His Word shall be known.

There are many other things that many of us fear;
Including lots of places we don't want to go near.

But fears are emotions that drift far away;
Whenever we face them and remember to pray.

TREES

TREES BEGIN AS LITTLE SEEDS;
THEN THEY SPROUT AMONG THE WEEDS.

THEY SEND THEIR ROOTS BENEATH THE SOIL;
IT'S ONLY THEN THAT THEY BEGIN THEIR TOIL.

THEY'RE BLOWN ABOUT BY WIND AND RAIN;
THEY HARDLY THINK THEY CAN WITHSTAND THE STRAIN.

BUT IN SPITE OF THAT THEY GROW STRONG AND TALL;
AND SOON THEIR LEAVES TURN COLORS IN THE FALL.

JESUS IS MUCH LIKE THE ROOT OF THE TREE;
WITHOUT HIS LOVE, WE JUST WOULDN'T BE.

THE CATHOLIC CHURCH IS LIKE THE TRUNK;
IF IT WASN'T FOR PETER WE'D ALL BE SUNK.

ALL CHRISTIAN CHURCHES FROM THE TRUNK SHOT OUT;
LIKE MANY BRANCHES WITHOUT A DOUBT.

BENEATH THE SOIL THE ROOT SENT OUT RUNNERS;
TO FORM THE ROOTS OF MANY OTHERS.

LIKE ISLAM, HINDUISM, AND BUDDHISM;
HOPEFULLY, WE'VE SEEN THE LAST OF FASCISM.

THE FALLING LEAF.

HI! MY NAME IS FREDDIE AND I'M AN OAK LEAF.
LAST SPRING I BRANCHED OUT FROM A TWIG.
I WAS FRESH AND GREEN AND FEISTY LIKE A THIEF.

I DIDN'T KNOW WHO I WAS – I THOUGHT I WAS A FIG.
I WITHSTOOD MANY WINDSTORMS AND GOT SOAKED BY THE RAIN.

BUT NOW THAT IT'S AUTUMN, I'M ALL RED AND GOLD;
THOUGH ALL THE OTHER LEAVES HAVE FALLEN,
I STILL REMAIN.

BUT SOON I WILL JOIN THEM ON THE GROUND WHERE IT'S COLD.

THE BUTTERFLY

HI! I'M CHARLIE THE WOOLY BLACK CATERPILLAR.
I JUST CRAWLED OUT FROM MY MOTHER'S NEST.

THE BRANCH THAT I'M CRAWLING ON IS A REAL THRILLER;
BUT AFTER EATING SO MANY LEAVES, I NEED A REST.

BUT NO MATTER HOW MUCH I EAT, I CAN'T SATISFY MY HUNGER;
EVERY DAY I GROW BIGGER AND FATTER.

LAST NIGHT IT POURED AND I FELT ALL THE THUNDER;
THEN I ASKED MYSELF DOES IT REALLY MATTER?

I TOLD MYSELF I'M JUST GOING TO ROLL MYSELF IN A LITTLE BALL;
THE NEXT THING I KNEW, I WAS SURROUNDED BY A SOFT, GREY SHELL.

BEFORE I KNEW IT THE SUMMER TURNED TO FALL;
SOMETHING CHANGED DEEP WITHIN ME,
BUT WHAT IT WAS I JUST COULDN'T TELL.

THEN SUDDENLY MY SHELL JUST FELL OFF ME;
NOW THAT I HAVE WINGS I'M SUDDENLY FREE –

TO FLY IN THE AIR FROM FLOWER TO FLOWER;
I BELIEVE IT IS GOD WHO GIVES ME THAT POWER.

I WONDER WHY?

Some birds have wings, but cannot fly....
I wonder why?
Some folks wish they could do new things, but never try...
I wonder why?

"I wonder why the earth is flat?" Columbus said one day!
But then he sailed to prove it is round, and it still is round today!

"I wonder why the lightning strikes?" said Franklin with delight!
But then off he went with key and string to launch his favorite kite!

"But ours is not to wonder why," some ancient Guru said!
"Ours is but to do or die!" And now that Guru's dead!

Sometimes it pays to wonder why-we do the things we do;
But some folks wonder all their lives, and never find a clue;
To why it is they've done shameful things, so here's my point of view:

They rise each day to go to work and make a lot of money.

Then the money comes, but goes so fast that it isn't funny!

When the bills come due-there's nothing left-so they wonder what to do!

A thought comes in-to escape let's say- and that's what they soon hope to do!

A pleasant picture in their mind is drawn by an artist full of darkness!

Ungodly deeds they soon perform-a quest to erase their sadness!

But with the morning LIGHT, the TRUTH creeps in….

and they see it all as madness!

The folly is to live our lives to serve our minds and bodies;

Instead of living for the LIGHT that shines….

with which our hope embodies!

God's Spirit of LOVE then becomes our Master;

And all the actions of our lives don't end up in disaster!

To live as soul is to be "born again,"

of fire and God's Spirit!

In spite of the turmoil in our lives and everything that comes with it!

To burn with LOVE-without conditions-in fact, to be at peace!

For then our lives become fulfilled…..

and all our doubts, fears and worries cease!

It's only now that I know why!

THE LITTLE FLOWER
AN ODE TO ST. THERESA OF LISIEUX!

"MY MISSION – TO MAKE GOD LOVED – WILL BEGIN AFTER MY DEATH..
I WILL LET FALL A SHOWER OF ROSES!"

ST. THERESA OF LISIEUX

HER BIOGRAPHY:

Therese Martin was the last of 9 children born to Louis and Zelie Martin on January 2nd, 1873 in the small town of Alencon, France. After her mother died when she was only 4 years old, the rest of her family spoiled her terribly since she was so cute! She was known to have a demanding spirit and wanted the best of everything. Then one day on Christmas Eve in 1886, when she was only 14 years old, she came to know the Lord in a very profound way. In short, she became "born again" as an adopted child of God!

From that moment on, she died to herself and became a new creature in Christ! Her powerful energy and sensitive, demanding spirit were turned toward love – the love for God – for all of humanity – and all of God's creation!

At 15 she entered the Carmelite convent in Lisieux and dedicated her whole life to God. She assumed the name of Sister Therese of the Child Jesus and the Holy Face. Although after several dark nights of sickness, doubt, and fear, she trusted that God would have mercy toward her because of His awesome love for her. Finally, 9 years later, she succumbed to the disease of tuberculosis and died on September 30th, 1897 at the young age of 24. While her family had gathered around her, she spoke the last words of her short, but devoted life to God: "My God, I love you!"

Sometime during those 9 years of her life, she wrote her autobiography entitled: "The Story of a Soul." She loved flowers and referred to herself as "the little flower of Jesus!" To this day she is revered throughout the world as "the little flower!"

She was loved and adored by so many people throughout the world for the many blessings she bestowed on them that she was canonized as a saint by Pope Pius XI on May 17th, 1925. She told the people that surrounded her during her short life on earth that her mission in life was to "spend her life in heaven doing good on planet earth!" Pope John Paul II was so impressed with her influence upon the hearts of the people of God's church and the many blessings that were showered down upon them through her divine intercession with God that in 1997 he declared her to be a "Doctor of the Church!"

Please don't pray to St. Therese! She prefers that we pray only to God! Yet she invites us to ask her to intercede for us to the Father for our behalf! So don't be surprised if a little puppy brings a rose to your doorstep!

THE EARLIEST EXPERIENCE OF LOVE IS PUPPY LOVE!

"Roses are red,
and violets are blue;
but soon they are dead,
and have nothing to do!

They live out their purpose,
when sent from above;
and their beauty and scent,
shower us with LOVE!

TIME

DO YOU HAVE THE CORRECT TIME?

Right now it's 3:15 in Massachusetts but 1:15 in California at the same time. Time is relative, they say, but relative to what? Relative to where in the world you happen to be at this moment! Time passes by from moment to moment, second to second, minute to minute, hour to hour, day to day, week to week, month to month, year to year, decade to decade, century to century, eons to eons, everlasting to everlasting.

Does it ever run out? No. Time is as eternal as God is eternal. Do you ever ask yourself the question: How much time does it take to accomplish a certain task?

How long will it take for all the humans in this world to become compassionate with one another? In the next century? Perhaps eons. The fact is that you can become compassionate right now. Do it anyway. If you do it now for others, perhaps others will return the favor. If it works for you, then it works for me. Praise God that I still have the time to write some more about the passage of time! Please don't forget to take TIME OUT to pray! But there's more! Read the next page if you have the time!

TIME...

Time ticks along one moment followed by another;

Time neither laughs nor cries as it brings birth to a child by it's mother;

Time is the unit by which all LIFE is measured;

Time is the only possession through which all storms are weathered;

Seconds, minutes, hours, days, months, and years;

Decades, and centuries come and go with joy and tears;

One day soon we will all be judged for whatever our crime;

But with CHRIST all is forgiven in the fullness of time!

ABOUT THE AUTHOR:

This book contains 33 poems written over the course of his lifetime by it's author, Mr. William Langen Burgoyne. Mr. Burgoyne resides in his apartment at 153A Blanchard Street in Gardner, Massachusetts. He received his bachelor's degree in Education at Norwich University in Northfield, Vermont and holds a Master's degree in Education from Worcester State College in Worcester, Massachusetts. He also holds a Master's degree in Counseling from Fitchburg State College in Fitchburg, Massachusetts.He is a divorced father of four children and lives alone.

THE ABOVE PICTURE WAS TAKEN AT THE CATHEDRAL OF THE PINES IN RINDGE, NEW HAMPSHIRE.

WILLIAM BURGOYNE IS THE PRESIDENT OF "RAM OF GOD" MINISTRIES WHICH IS LOCATED AT HILLSIDE GARDENS IN GARDNER, MA. FOR FURTHER INFORMATION, PLEASE CHECK OUT OUR WEB-SITE AT *WWW.FAMOUSAUTHOR.ORG*.